Paper Chains

poems by

Loretta Oleck

Finishing Line Press
Georgetown, Kentucky

Paper Chains

*Dedicated to all forced to flee their homes due to violence
and persecution; in honor of their fortitude and courage.*

"We lost our home, which means the familiarity of daily life. We lost our
occupation, which means the confidence that we are of some use in this
world. We lost our language, which means
the naturalness of reactions, the simplicity of gestures,
the unaffected expression of feelings."
—Hannah Arendt

"It is the obligation of every person born in a safer room to open
the door when someone in danger knocks."
—Dina Nayeri

Copyright © 2020 by Loretta Oleck
ISBN 978-1-64662-137-8 First Edition
All rights reserved under International and Pan-American Copyright Conventions. No part of this book may be reproduced in any manner whatsoever without written permission from the publisher, except in the case of brief quotations embodied in critical articles and reviews.

ACKNOWLEDGMENTS

I wish to express my grateful acknowledgment to the following publications in which these poems first appeared:

Cultural Weekly ~~ "Fathi," "Samina," and "Outlines"
Right Hand Pointing #69 ~~ "Sharar" published first as "Songs" and later included in "Songs From the Black Hole," Finishing Line Press, 2016
Laurel Review ~~ "Rima"
DoveTales: Writing for Peace ~~ "Samina," "Bore Snake," "Entitled"
Burning House Press ~~ "Meeting Frank"
A Pact Press Anthology ~~ "Laya and Aseel" published in "We Refugees"

Deep gratitude to the strong and inspiring men, women, and children living at Ritsona Refugee Camp in Greece, all of who endured treacherous journeys in their quest to find a safe haven. Thank you to Lighthouse Relief for offering me the opportunity to volunteer at Ritsona, and to all the dedicated volunteers and staff. To Linton Suttner, I offer loving appreciation for supplying author photos, designing the book cover, and for providing feedback. Thank you to Ron Egatz and Jonathon Blunk for their editing and focused comments and blurbs, to Alexis Rhone-Fancher and Cynthia Atkins for their thoughtful readings and poetic reviews, Mara Mills in deciding that the poems here within were worthy inspirations for a theater production by the Studio Theater In Exile, and thank you to Finishing Line Press, Christen Kincaid, and Leah Maines. And of course gratitude and love to my beautiful family.

Publisher: Leah Maines
Editor: Christen Kincaid
Cover Art: Loretta Oleck
Author Photo: Linton Suttner
Cover Design: Linton Suttner

Printed in the USA on acid-free paper.
Order online: www.finishinglinepress.com
 also available on amazon.com

Author inquiries and mail orders:
Finishing Line Press
P. O. Box 1626
Georgetown, Kentucky 40324
U. S. A.

Table of Contents

New York to Ritsona
Full Moon 1
Meeting Frank 2
Body Bag 4
From A Distance 5

Children
Lone Moths 6
Climbing the Fence 7
Lightening Bolt /Moonif 8
Baby Tigers /Achmed and Hassan 9
Distraction /Sayid 10
Blackbirds Flying Out a Hungry Mouth /Zeinah 12
Mothers Fold Sorrows into Laundry /Laya and Aseel 14
Bore Snake 15
Paper Chains 17
Wild Toad /Suhair 18
Outlines 20
Beauty /Janna 21
Clock Strikes Five /Fathi 22

Women
Daughter /Sharar 23
Blood Moon /Bana 24
Special /Sara 25
Broken Bristle Brushes /Samina 26
Tent 574 27
Darling /Nooda 28
Skeleton Dancer /Farhah 30
Tough Man /Iman 31
Bark and Blood /Sheera 32
Waiting /Rima 33
The Butterfly Effect 34
Liminality 35
We 36

New York to Ritsona

Full Moon

I am here in the light of a full moon
while *that* is happening over *there*,
across the sea, in someone else's
backyard, under someone else's
full moon—

a full moon shaped like a barrel-bomb.

Meeting Frank

Flying from New York,
I am seated next to a man
named Frank.

35,000 feet in the air,
high above sea level,
far from surging waves—

a tsunami of tents swelling
inside a refugee camp
on a burned-out military base—

a different kind of sea,
one I have yet to witness.

Frank says,
To make a difference, open your heart.

I once believed it was that simple
before I flew across the ocean, brimming
with conviction, questioning contradictions
impossible to resolve—

why do I fly so seamlessly, so shamelessly,
from one country to the next, while others
are turned away at borders?

I once believed it was that simple
before I struck up a friendly conversation
with a stranger named Frank,
before the seatbelt sign blinked on.

Frank should know we are always
in someone else's hands.

An open heart won't grant asylum,
open borders, stop bombings, or create
a gentler river of wind in the atmosphere.

The only thing to do when caught
in turbulence is find that sweet spot.

Fly, like the captain with intent to steer
through tumult.

Fly, as fast possible while burning
the least amount of fuel.

Body Bag

The red, white and blue carry-on tumbles
from the overhead bin. Handles tangled
together like wrestling arms.

The belly of the bag bursts open
splashing across the aisle—collective
bigotry, racism, xenophobia.

A shedding of skin—
first, second, third generation skin,
stand up for your rights, freedom
of speech, Babylon crashing down,
carry-on falling from the overhead bin
trampling everything-to-win kind of skin.

I was told,
Beware the snakes at the camp.
They slither between the tents. Handling
opaque ones will damage fresh skin
growing beneath the old. These snakes
spew poison up to 8 feet with 90% accuracy.

No need to worry about baggage
weighing me down. No need to worry
about crossing borders or handling snakes.

My U.S passport rests safely in my pocket.

From a Distance

An NGO worker drives me up
a windy road, past anemic farms
on our way to the refugee camp.

Makeshift tents are marooned
in dusty olive groves.

A mother lifts her naked daughter
from a pail of water, skinny
as a pine needle.

*They've hacked the branches
of olive trees,* says the NGO worker.
They were cold and needed kindling.

A mother curls on the ground, skirt
bunches above her knees, bare feet
and calves caked with mud, arms drape
over an infant with tousled hair.

As we speed by, mothers and children
promptly vanish from view, not unlike
newspaper images chucked to the curb
for recycling.

Children

Lone Moths

Morse code—
dots and dashes dusted
on a lone moth's wings,
tapping and scratching
on tent walls.

Hope is barely audible.

Climbing the Fence

Unexpectedly, children climb the fence
and dart like baby bulls, quick as bullets,
into the *Children's Friendly Space.*

Some barefoot. Some in mismatched
sandals, all dusty-faced.

The fence is high, but even toddlers
find ways to scale its heights.

An angry boy throws stones, others
scatter in silence.

No squeals of protest. No laughter.
Just a scrambling of little feet
clambering this way and that
like mimes in a silent motion picture.

But it is real. And so am I—

having traveled here to help refugees
while also running from my own rising
swell of losses. My heart ground coarsely
into peppered debris. The children tiptoe
so not to trample over its remains.

I stand with my hand on a gate, ready
to push it open or closed like a hinge
on the face of a compass.

The children are not interested in gates
that open and close nor in cardinal points
nor in my heart's wreckage.

They are only interested in climbing
back and forth over the fence with no one
to dictate which side to choose.

Lightning Bolt
Moonif

Owl-eyed Moonif stares into the sun.
A reel of images tumbling through his mind—

crumbling walls, a cousin caught in the crosshairs,
a neighbor drowning at sea.

His tiny body is a twisted bonsai tree artificially dwarfed
into a cramped container of earth, over-saturated with fear.

Tears spark in his coal eyes hemmed with lashes so long
they have grown into a tourniquet tight around his limbs—
a snaking cocoon propping him up so he doesn't collapse.

One day, he shows up with a lightning bolt shaved
into his hair. Fierce rumblings of an armored truck
echo from a pit deep inside his belly. Rounds of artillery
spit out warning whistles with each inhale of measured breath.

And that lightning bolt on the side of his head strikes
so sharply it strips all darkness from the night
like a bandage torn from an open wound.

Baby Tigers
Achmed and Hassan

The little ones arrive speaking
Kurdish and Arabic, glazed over,
bewildered when the volunteers
use English words.

Achmed pulls plastic animals
from a bin, lining up the tigers
in neat rows from smallest to tallest.

He beams—
the first smile I have seen.

Hassan, a boy wearing two left sandals,
spits in Achmed's eye. A droplet flies
onto my cheek, dripping like a tear.

Hassan points to the spit,
and surprisingly yells in English,
Blood!

Then he kicks over Achmed's
tidy row of tigers.

I place my hand on Hassan's shoulder.
He jerks away and sprints to the fence
ripping down children's artwork taped
onto planks of wood.

Achmed is crying, fist pounding tigers.

I squat beside him, line them up once again,
one by one, but now he swats them away
with mounting rage. Howling hard.

Every moment I am with these children
is an attempt to construct order amid turmoil.
Every moment is an attempt to distract
predator from prey.

Infliction never ends.
Even baby tigers need to eat.

Distraction
Sayid

Sayid wears army fatigues
and refuses to abide by rules.
To him, volunteers are fools.
They cannot regulate nor rein in
the explosive energy of so many
stateless children.

To Sayid, volunteers are yielding.
Drippy. He points to them and says,
You are soft-boiled eggs.

He learns to become
their biggest distraction,
their number one attraction.

They teach him lyrics like,
I can't get no satisfaction.
And when he sings in perfect pitch
the volunteers ditch whatever
they are doing and say,

You're gonna be a somebody someday.

The children sit in a circle learning signals:
pointer-finger crossed over lips = *quiet voice*
arms crisscrossed over chest = *safe hands*

But not Sayid.

He pulls silly faces
and bops from side to side
in rhythmic hip-hop moves.
He grabs a crayon and draws a bomb
plummeting from a darkened sky.

He bangs on the back of a cardboard box
smashing it with his fists.
He balances high above the ground,
tippy-toe on top of the fence—

a wild boy gyrating his hips,
mesmerizing volunteers who easily forget
he is a just a child in grave danger
of slipping from such great heights.

Blackbirds Flying Out a Hungry Mouth
    Zeinah

Zeinah is a filthy-faced little girl,
with a nest of twisted twigs resting
upon her head like a crown.

Did I say twigs?

I meant to say lice.
A nest of lice.
A hive, actually.

I saw twenty blackbirds spring
from her thirsty mouth.

Did I say blackbirds?

I meant to say teeth
like rotted apple pits
and moths of every color
in twitchy flight fluttering
from fidgety fingertips

and bare feet kicking up dust
on a bone dry path between rows
of tents sharp as crocodile teeth.

She looks like my daughter's
best friend, Ashley Brown—
the girl who lived in a crowded
condo before moving to a mansion
in New Jersey.

Zeinah and Ashley could be sisters.

But there is no crown of twigs
on Ashley's head. No hives of lice.
No blackbirds flying out a hungry mouth.
No moths scattering from fingertips.
No rotted teeth like apple pits.

Just a mansion in New Jersey
with a kidney-shaped pool
in a manicured backyard,
seldom if ever used.

Mothers Fold Sorrows into Laundry
    Laya and Aseel

Laya and Aseel, 13 years old,
need to be babied but it is too late
for babying.

Mothers fold sorrows into laundry.

The girls suck stones, imagining
they are peppermint candies.

They steal crayons, plastic beads,
and bits of string.

They slap the cheeks of children,
then cry, pretending to be struck first.

Mothers fold sorrows into laundry.

In the evenings, Laya and Aseel
wedge their sleepy siblings
into wobbly strollers, then push them
round the tents, the distribution center,
and the latrines.

Their dark eyes remain focused
on this journey of circles, on this labyrinth
with no beginning and no end.

Mothers pin sweaters and slacks
to tangled webs of clothing lines.

Stolen trinkets—
stubs of crayons, random beads, bits
of string, an occasional cat-eyed marble
tumble out from pockets like gems.

Bore Snake

You are a young boy smudging red paint across your cheeks.
Pale palms drumming on a cardboard box as you run
through the camp with a twisted branch like a rifle
flung over your skinny little shoulders.

The roar of war pulses through your veins—
a war that took your artist father who was also once a wild boy
sucking loose mint and lemon and marching through the brush
beyond his house where he once belonged.

Your mother knew your father hummed when he was nervous;
a warm but tense hum under the sheets, with mango juice
dripping down flesh, sticky on lips.

Now your mother secretly carries ripe mango memories
and craves red pistachios, knowing that the hue of cherry
staining her fingers will distract her from the bitter bite of blood.

She hopes her husband will forever sleep with his cheek pressed
like a leaf against a soft patch of her blue hijab.

And you, the eldest son, now imagine your father is spreading
a message of hope with a sweep of his paintbrush.
But the only brush that seems to matter in this war is a bore snake
to keep a gun's barrel carbon free.

When an explosion echoed in the distance, your mother
dropped a pomegranate flooding the floor with a stream
of crimson pearls and juice-blushed skin.

She knew he was gone. Her husband. Your father.
Under ruins. Clutching fragments of rock to his chest.
The same way he cupped his wife's breasts.
The same way he cradled you as an infant.
The same way he held a slippery sweet mango pit.

When you declare your father as lucky to be spared
stateless status, your mother slaps you on the side
of the head and says,

Forgiveness rises from the pearls of a pomegranate just as easily as from the venom of a bore snake.

Paper Chains

Children are clad in Rolling Stones tee shirts,
purple boots, flower leggings, army fatigues,
paper princess crowns.

Striking children dance the Macarena,
parrot foreign words, mock teachers,
bead necklaces, ride bikes, splash water,
kick balls.

Some children steal bananas.
Some scribble magic markers
across each other's arms.
Some share crayons.
Some don't.

Children.
Like my own.
Like yours.

They like to cut colored paper
into long strips, loop and glue them
together to create paper chains.

They make chains so long they snake
around the pine trees, zigzag over muddy
pathways, wind tight knots between the tents.

They make chains just so they can break them.

Wild Toad
    Suhair

Understand, these days are not normal.

A wild toad hops into Suhair's open mouth.
She becomes possessed—kicking down
the school's gate, biting her teacher's forearm,
scraping skin off another child's ear.

Blood slakes earth's thirst.

Graffiti on decaying walls surrounds the perimeter
of this camp with scrawled words—
hope revenge hope revenge.

Suhair's screams are so shrill others freeze
waiting to see what will happen next.

Understand, these days are not normal.

The wild toad spills out of Suhair's mouth,
becomes stuck in the mud, struggles to stay alive,
then vanishes in sludge.

Suhair's father is angry his daughter has caused
such a commotion. He punches her in the face.

Suhair, with a swollen black eye, wallops a teacher
over the head with a plastic bucket. If the teacher
writes an incident report, Suhair will be beaten,
again.

Her father never intended to hurt her. He intended
to teach her to keep her mouth shut, stay out
of trouble, and keep away from wild toads
that croak when frightened.

Understand, these days are not normal.

Lines are blurred between grief and rage,
love and fear, protection and hope.

These days, ears remain cocked like loaded guns straining to hear the faintest whistle of all things familiar.

Outlines

The children draw outlines of their bodies,
then sketch depictions of their feelings inside.

One boy illustrates Superman.
I am tough, he says, flexing his little arm muscles.
He scrawls the word *strong* on each bicep.

One dark-haired dark-skinned girl draws a princess
with blond hair and blue eyes, then names her *Lydia,*
the name of a Swedish human-rights worker.

Write—I am beautiful. She hands me a crayon
like handing me a question.

One quiet boy depicts a clock as his face—
time imprinted inside his features, worn like camouflage
over impermanence. Then, he draws a zigzag across
his forehead, slicing through the hands of time.

One angry boy smudges black across his outline,
crumbles the paper, shoves it fully into his mouth,
gobbling himself whole, destroying all evidence
of his existence.

Beauty
Janna

Janna looks as familiar as my little sister,
flashing a toothy smile with a lot of gum.
Her hair is twisty black licorice cascading
over her cheeks and chest. She wears spandex
pants and a Beauty-and-the-Beast tee shirt.

Stealthily, she tiptoes up behind me, pressing
sticky palms over my eyes, leaning in so close
her hair falls over my shoulders, making it
impossible to know if they are her curls or mine.

Guess who? She laughs. What's my name?

It's you! Janna, with the big smile!

But I'm not sure if it is really Janna.
She might be my little sister. Or my cousin.
Or me.

She drapes her arms around my waist and we walk
to her tent where her mother, who looks just like Janna,
and just like my mother too, serves red lentils, warm rice,
and instant coffee.

In the dark, after the volunteers pack into cars to leave,
the camp begins to stir. Tents rouse like nocturnal animals
under a string of bright stars.

Janna and other children slip away to scour the grounds
searching for forgotten plastic beads hidden among pebbles,
buried beneath the dusty earth.

Night after night, prized booty is strung into ornate patterns.
Night after night, children create beauty out of nothing.

Clock Strikes Five
    Fathi

Fathi is easily overlooked, showing one face but owning another. One face says, *don't touch me*. The other one is the face of a clock striking 5 pm—the time when Fathi arrives daily at the *Children's Friendly Space* to seek me out.

Most children don't attach to volunteers because they come and go, leaving every few weeks, reminding the children of all their other losses.

Fathi is no different. His mother is dead. His grandparents left behind in Aleppo. He lives, now, in a tent with his father and uncle. They sleep on thin quilts atop plastic tarps, choosing to keep their tent sparse so it will not feel permanent.

In the corner, a scorpion hides in a crate of red apples.

Fathi winds and knots a colorful beaded necklace around my neck.

He gives me a pocketbook cut out from cardboard, stuffed with paper stars and hearts.

I wear the necklace daily, and although I wedge the pocketbook between hard journal pages for safekeeping, the hearts and stars tumble out, everywhere—

forging a trail, like in a fairytale, leading me straight back to Fathi to say my goodbye.

Women

Daughter
Sharar

Her daughter was born with songs
that would fly away in winter
dangling like floppy fish
from beaks of geese
who one by one
accidentally
dropped
them
into
the
sea.

Blood Moon
> *Bana*

Time inside this camp dangles
like a limp clock wrung out to dry.
The art of waiting bleeds from the
deepest wound in the darkest sky.

One night, there is a meteor shower.
Plump stars splatter like ripened apricots,
like Aleppo's sky before it melted
into liquid mercury.

A volunteer tells Bana,

When the full moon is tinged ruby,
it is called a blood moon.

Bana gazes at the suspended red disc—
a medallion dangling from a black cloth
over night's chest; a big heart thumping

like the first time she placed her palm
to her husband's torso and she felt his thin
bones dipping inwards under tight skin—
a bowl in which to stir cool rain and fresh tears.

She has never stroked another man's chest.
She never will.

Now her husband does not want to touch her.
He does not want her to touch him.
He will no longer gaze into her eyes
for fear he will see what he has since become
and be reminded of all that has been lost.

Bana searches the sky and finds no medallion
hanging from a black cloth over night's chest.

A blood moon is not a good thing
and her husband's concave bones
no longer house his heart.

Special
> *Sara*

Sara has the nicest tent because she is the squeaky wheel.

Come inside! she says in perfect English, serving licorice tea and red lentils to the volunteers. Her home is a showcase for the happy refugee, and volunteers feel free to enter without knocking.

Salome. Kayfa Haluk? ask volunteers wearing vests bearing NGO names. They hope a few phrases of muddled Arabic might bridge the culture gap.

The volunteers give a bicycle to Sara's son. Now he becomes a member of the wild pack who rides in circles round the camp.

But Sara knows her son is neither fierce nor rowdy. He is a clever one quickly learning that to be the wild boy from the poster family of well-adjusted and grateful refugees will serve him well.

Volunteers wave to him, take his photo, bring him apples and feel less heart-broken about his circumstance because this handsome young boy rides a bicycle like any other handsome young boy on any suburban street anywhere.

Sara knows her son is the only wild boy who struggles to keep his balance when lifting his hands off the handlebars. She knows he will try to do it anyway to belong to the pack.

She knows that while she entertains eager volunteers, her son is pedaling hard with hands high in the air. She knows one day a corner will be cut too sharply, and everything will come crashing down.

Broken Bristle Brushes
Samina

Samina worked as a landscape painter in Aleppo.

Now, she stands amid a field of tents. The irony not lost on her that here, at a refugee camp, there is an endless supply of canvas.

Her shelves of colored paints are buried deep under rubble, splattered across shards of bone and mixed with shattered vials of turpentine and broken bristle brushes.

And flesh buried, too, bathed in a wash of paints the color of plump berries and springtime. Lush earth. Emerald. Lime. Sublime hues too fertile, too vital, to be found running through the cold veins of a refugee camp.

Nothing and no one has stayed the same.
The remains of her paint camouflage the dead.

She would no longer recognize friends if she saw them.

Tent 574

She comes from a place where ammo jingles
in pockets like coins, children are curled up
caterpillars, and her wounded face has warped
into someone else's.

Gunpowder cheeks hide tears like a mourning
cloth. Hatred is hatred passed from mothers'
milk to babies' lips.

Here, she is hidden.
Here, she is nameless.

Known only by her tent 574.
A bare and barren tent. Not like tent 413
with its soft mattress and patchwork coverlet.

She swallows pinches of her own sweat
to remember what she tastes like.

Here, she is a stranger to others.
Here, she is a stranger to herself.

She is a woman who froze when artillery fire
ricocheted between the peach-painted walls
of what was once her home.

She lives here now because borders are closed,
stewing in hatred that dogs her like a shadow.

Hope is a bulletproof vest but she is too angry
to wear one.

Darling
Nooda

Nooda's husband holds her hands at night,
light as a feather, kisses each fingertip,
whispers, *be patient.*

Although they speak Arabic, he calls her *darling*
in English, enjoying the way *darling* rolls off
his tongue.

And it makes her feel young. And it gives him hope.

Cold rain dilutes thick mud, leaving a steady stream
of brown water rushing into their tent. A black snake
hides under a pile of baby diapers.

Her husband mimics the wild boar sniffing around
the nearby latrines. The boar grunts. Her husband grunts.
Nooda cups her hand over her mouth, stifling laughter
so those in adjacent tents don't hear.

To Nooda, what is most strange about this refugee camp
is that there are no birds. No birds in trees. No birds in sky.
Not even one.

Red Cross, Lighthouse Relief, Echo, I Am You—
NGO's volunteers come and go with macramé-hearts,
papier-mâché-hearts, turning-away-hearts, full-generous-
hearts, hearts-of-feathers, hearts-of-stone.

Nooda is made from stars. Nooda is made from bones.

Her husband says, *Habibi. Darling. Ahabak. I love you.*

The graying moon casts peppery shadows on a push-me-
pull-you earth, on a world plump with promise
yet tearing at the seams.

Stateless people dragging silenced dreams.

Nooda holds her husband under a scratchy sheet and asks,

Might the wisdom in the gray moon and in the gray locks hidden under hijabs braid a path towards peace?

Skeleton Dancer
    Farhah

Farhah scoops up dusty earth
from the dry-as-bone path.

Kiss it. Lick it. Love it.

She and her daughter are alive.

They are alive even if forgotten.
Even if forsaken. Even if all hope
is filleted from the ribs of nameless
animals.

She holds her daughter's hennaed hand,
fingers longer and colder than her own.
A grown woman's hand. A numb hand.
No, not another corpse's hand.

They are alive. As alive as the volunteers
who smoke incessantly—incense swirling
from cheery-cherry lips making love
to English words. Words that taste sweet
on the tongue:

safety liberty home safety liberty home

Glossy lips whorled into a world of smiles
because these volunteers, all of them,
have countries and homes to return to.

Her daughter used to push aside the window-
shade to dance with her reflection in the glass.
Now there are no windows, just rows of canvas
tents numbered into the thousands.

They are alive. Even though her daughter
has become a skeleton dancer, a lamb to
slaughter, a barren-eyed, stymied-hearted
daughter hiding wild waves under a muted
head scarf. A fleshless girl who cannot bear
to wear another scar.

Tough Man
> *Iman*

Her husband sits shirtless inside their tent,
with the words *hard life* scrawled over his flesh.

His chest muscles flinch when she hugs him,
and his cold eyes remain half-mast.

Hardness is his story, the one she hears
loud and clear in his silence.

Even here, while dying on the inside, she tries
to see herself as a peaking pink gardenia opening
with the fragrance of readiness, ignoring all signs
of danger.

Her husband grips a hunter's knife. Tough man.
Tough but no longer steady enough to trim her stem
into the perfect angle to quench her thirst.

No blame. He lost his business, family, job, friends,
voice, home, heart.

No blame when she tells him she lost just as much,
and his face reddens with rage, and he slices open
the skein of her cocoon, and she emerges in a tangle
of dying petals and straining blossoms.

No blame when she says,
Falling and failing can still be overcome.

No blame when her words prompt her husband
to clench the knife tighter and with the precision
of a stateless surgeon, he clips her wings.

This is the price he pays for the sins of their country.
This is the price she pays for loving him.

Bark and Blood
Sheera

Star leaves floated
between
brambles and moss—

she searched for beauty
where ever she could
find it.

Bark and blood
flowed through
the Queiq River—

shrill slivers of treble
in a troubling song.

Bow against rock.
Breath amid shock.

Melancholy melody
rearranging her beliefs
about humanity.

Naked parks stripped
of trees. Wood used
to fuel fire.

After the trees were gone,
school desks were chopped
into kindling—

wooden legs, emptied
drawers, smudgy knobs,

heaped into piles until there
was nothing left to burn
but bones.

Waiting
Rima

Red hands. Restless hands. Blood painted along
the ridges of her ribs and down the ladder of her spine—
rigid in the teasing tight light under the cover of night.

There are no answers living inside the hush and hum
of shadows. She has stopped asking why. Stopped
wondering if she should crawl out of tent 604 or stay
inside and doze all day.

There is nowhere to go. Seven months of nothingness.

Waiting has taken on new meaning—
powerlessness.

Her blood lies stagnant in her veins—
blood that had once tasted sweetest while washing
through the heart of another.

Now, there is only the bitter bite of tossing alone,
lying on hard ground tangled in a single sheet.

It's as if she is the only one alive at this camp, at dawn,
holding back the urge to run, to scream, to punch—

surging urges smudged away with war paint smeared
across her cheeks and lips, erasing her face from her face.

She is living a life of waiting now. No more wanting.
Only camouflage can save her.

The Butterfly Effect

Babies conceived in war—
winged beauties emerging from a murky mess
from the darkness of a shaking sheath.

Babies breath have the surging might
to crack open the midnight sky.

Every flap-winged flutter in a refugee camp
stirs up a tornado thousands of miles away.

There is great power in innocence.

New mothers come for their daily rations
of powdered infant formula, even though
the volunteers advise them to breastfeed.

It is healthier and cheaper, they say.

No. We are not animals.

One day, babies' howls will rise up
fierce enough to pierce through stone,
sharp enough to cut through barbed wire.

Worn-out women walk the margins
of the camp. There is nowhere else to go.

Dead.   Space.

How many mothers, and mothers of mothers,
walk the edges, borders, limits of camps?

How many babies are conceived in war?

What is the lifespan of a butterfly?

Liminality

They are neither living nor dead,
existing in a no-man's land,
in animated suspension,
betwixt and between.

At night, when this camp is devoid
of light, wild boars descend.
Greek boars, mythological monsters
barreling through tents, avoiding those
whose scent leaves behind
a limbo trail—

ordinary people finding themselves
in extraordinary circumstances,
trying to separate freedom from fate,
impoverished riffs from improvised
twangs on an oud with broken strings.

The pit and pulse of fear.
The pang of hunger.

They sleep where they want,
whenever they want. With little else
to do, they carefully measure their days
by the heavy weight and want of waiting.

Their nights too are calculated by grunts
of wild boars on the hunt, and beating herds
of broken hearts killing time.

We

I am them.
They are me.
We are all
one heartbeat away
from becoming
who we never
thought we were.

www.ingramcontent.com/pod-product-compliance
Lightning Source LLC
LaVergne TN
LVHW041556070426
835507LV00011B/1122